This Book
Belongs to

puzzle 1

puzzle 2

puzzle 3

puzzle 4

puzzle 6

puzzle 7

puzzle 8

puzzle 10

puzzle 11

puzzle 12

puzzle 14

puzzle 15

puzzle 16

puzzle 18

puzzle 20

puzzle 22

puzzle 25

puzzle 26

puzzle 27

puzzle 28

puzzle 29

puzzle 30

puzzle 32

puzzle 33

puzzle 34

puzzle 35

puzzle 36

puzzle 37

puzzle 40

puzzle 41

puzzle 44

puzzle 45

puzzle 46

puzzle 47

puzzle 48

puzzle 49

puzzle 50

puzzle 51

puzzle 52

puzzle 53

puzzle 55

puzzle 56

puzzle 58

puzzle 59

puzzle 60

puzzle 61

puzzle 62

puzzle 63

puzzle 66

puzzle 67

puzzle 68

puzzle 71

puzzle 72

puzzle 74

puzzle 75

puzzle 76

puzzle 80

solution 1

solution 2

solution 3

solution 4

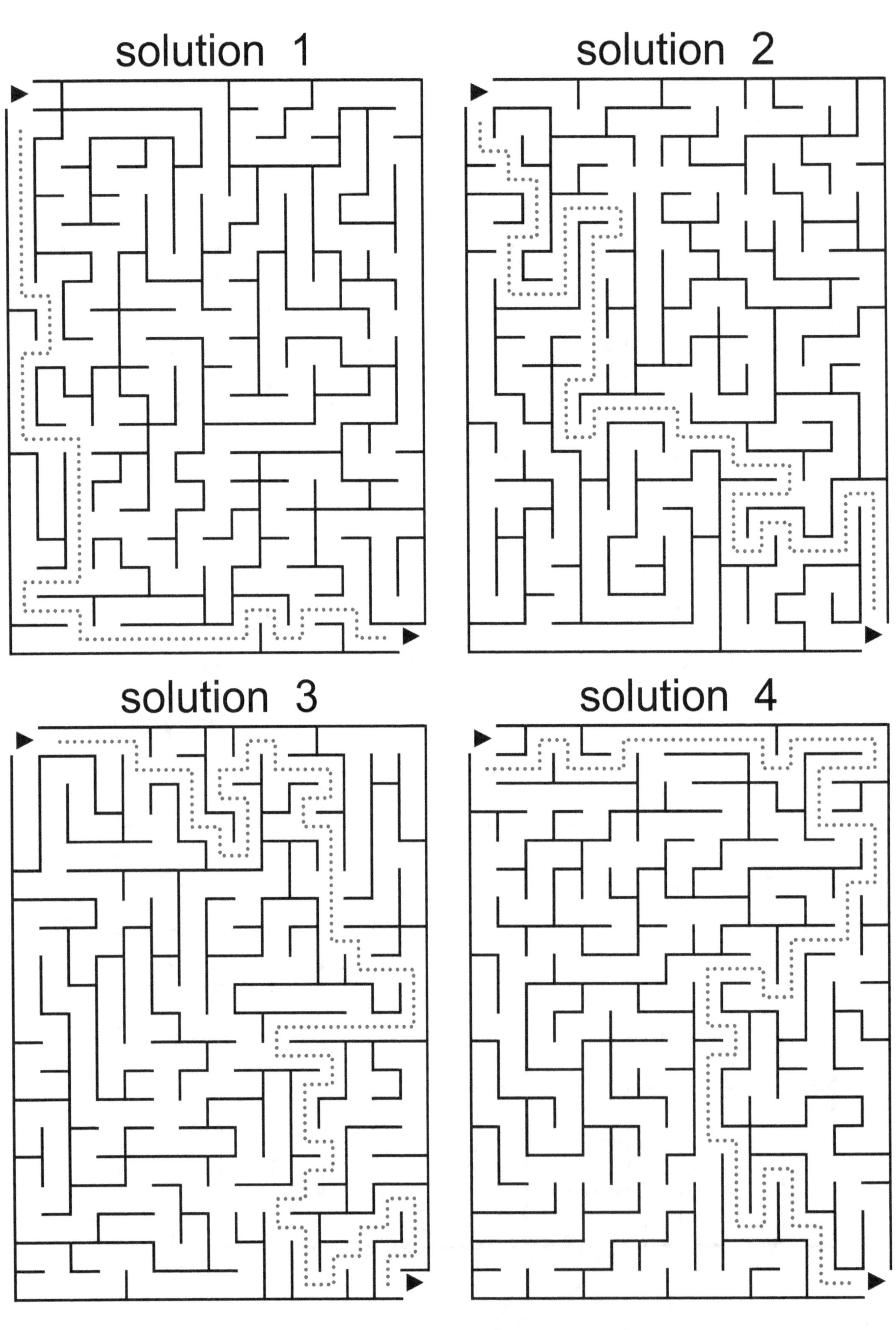

solution 5

solution 6

solution 7

solution 8

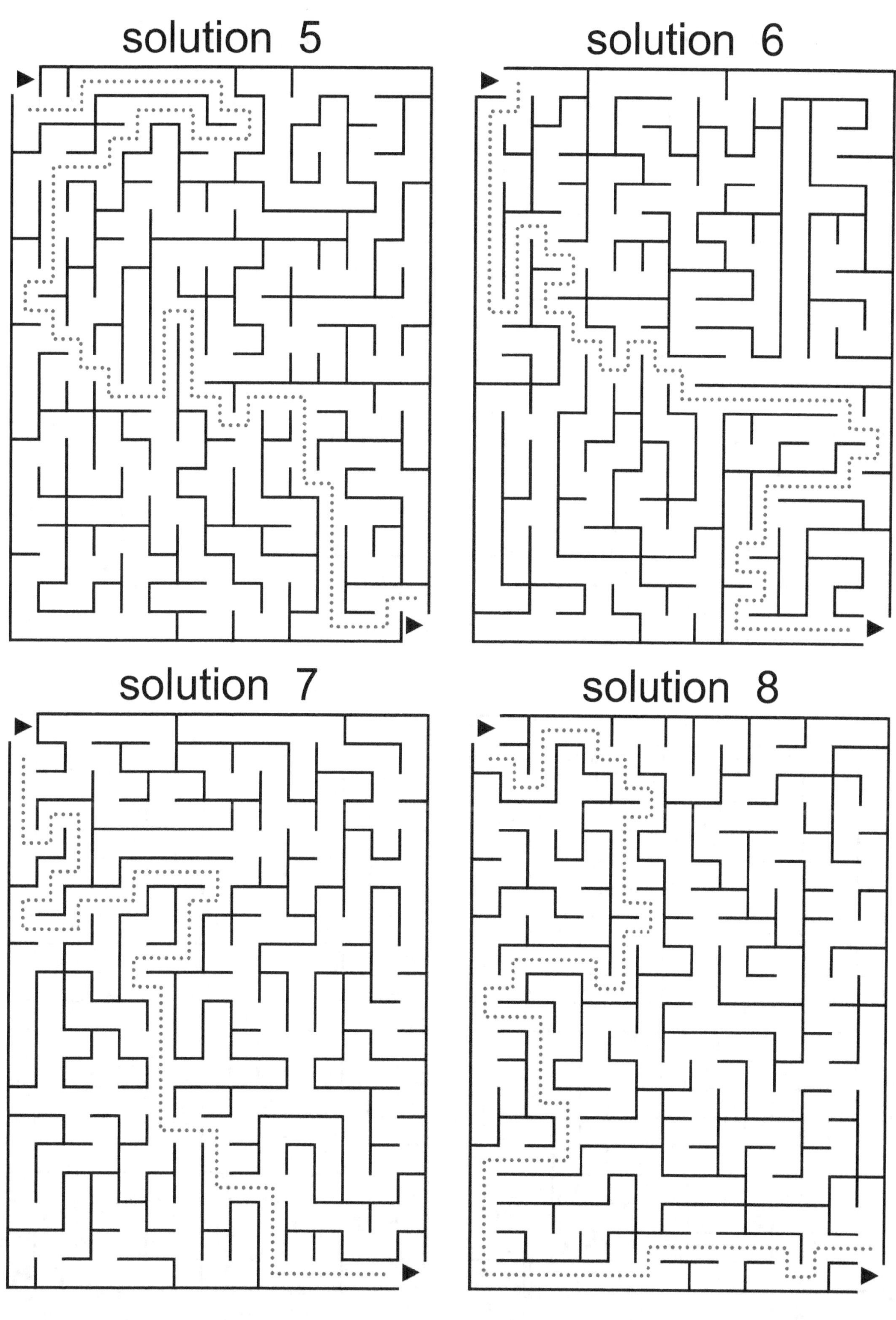

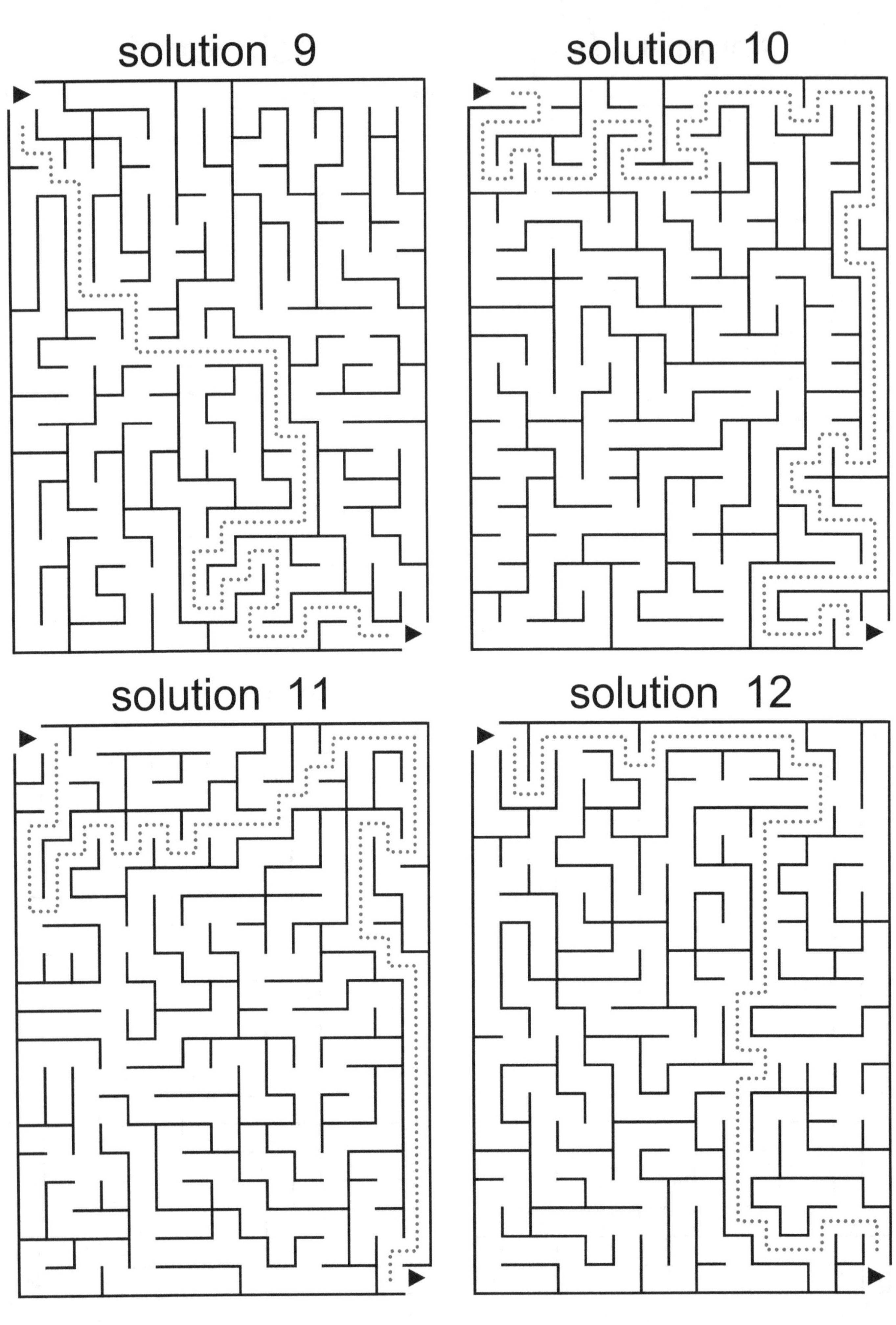

solution 9
solution 10
solution 11
solution 12

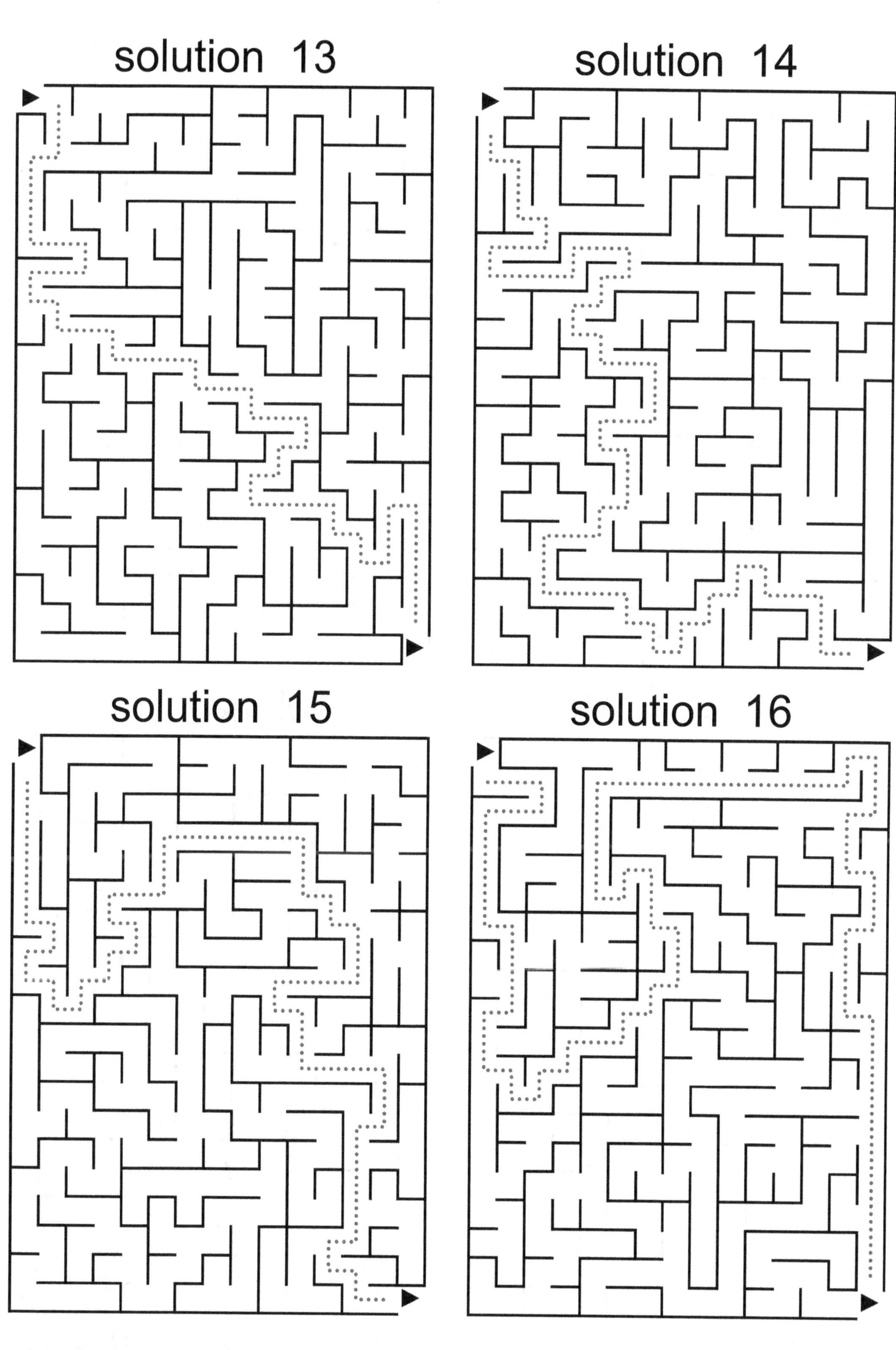

solution 13
solution 14
solution 15
solution 16

solution 17

solution 18

solution 19

solution 20

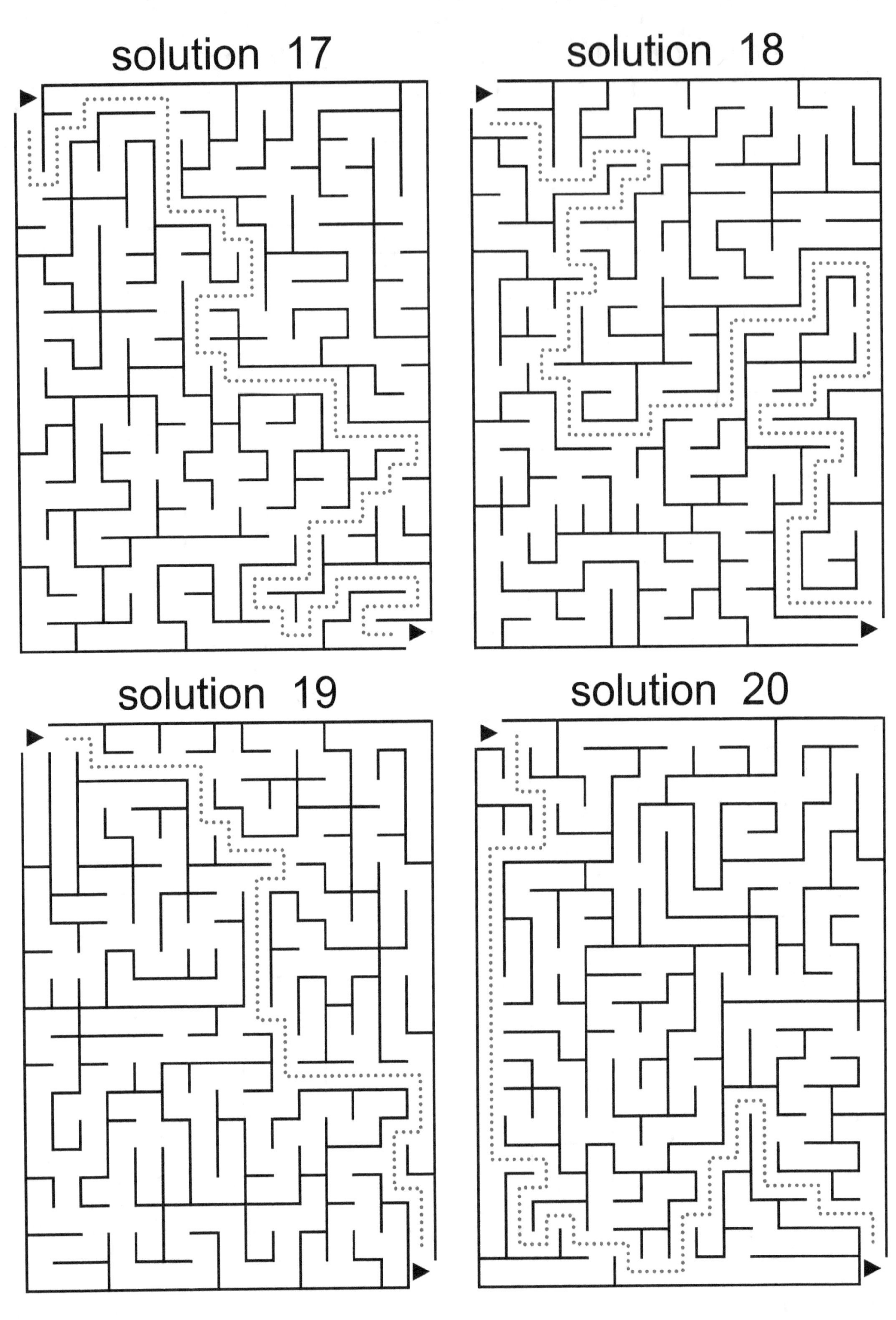

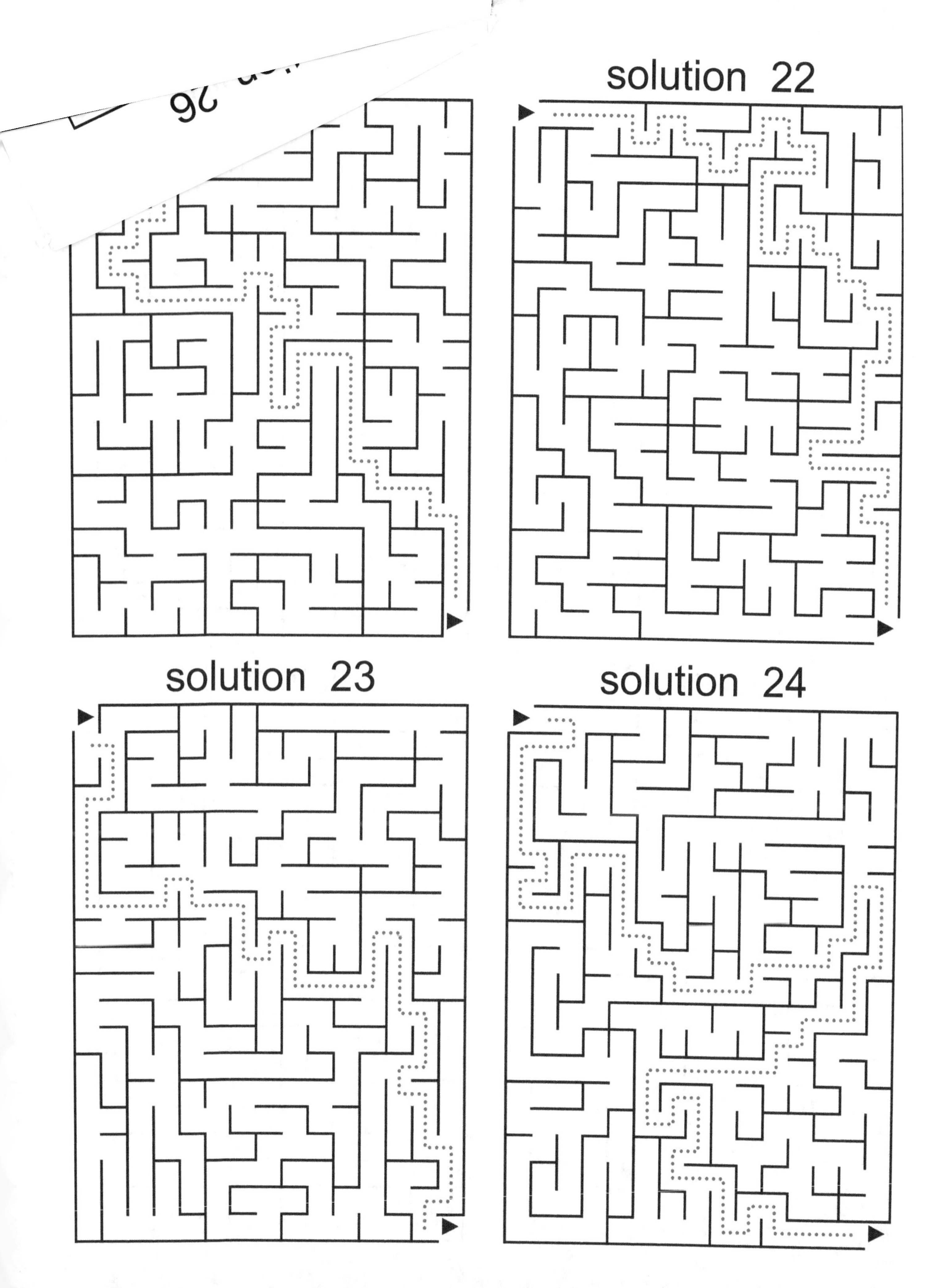

solution 22
solution 23
solution 24

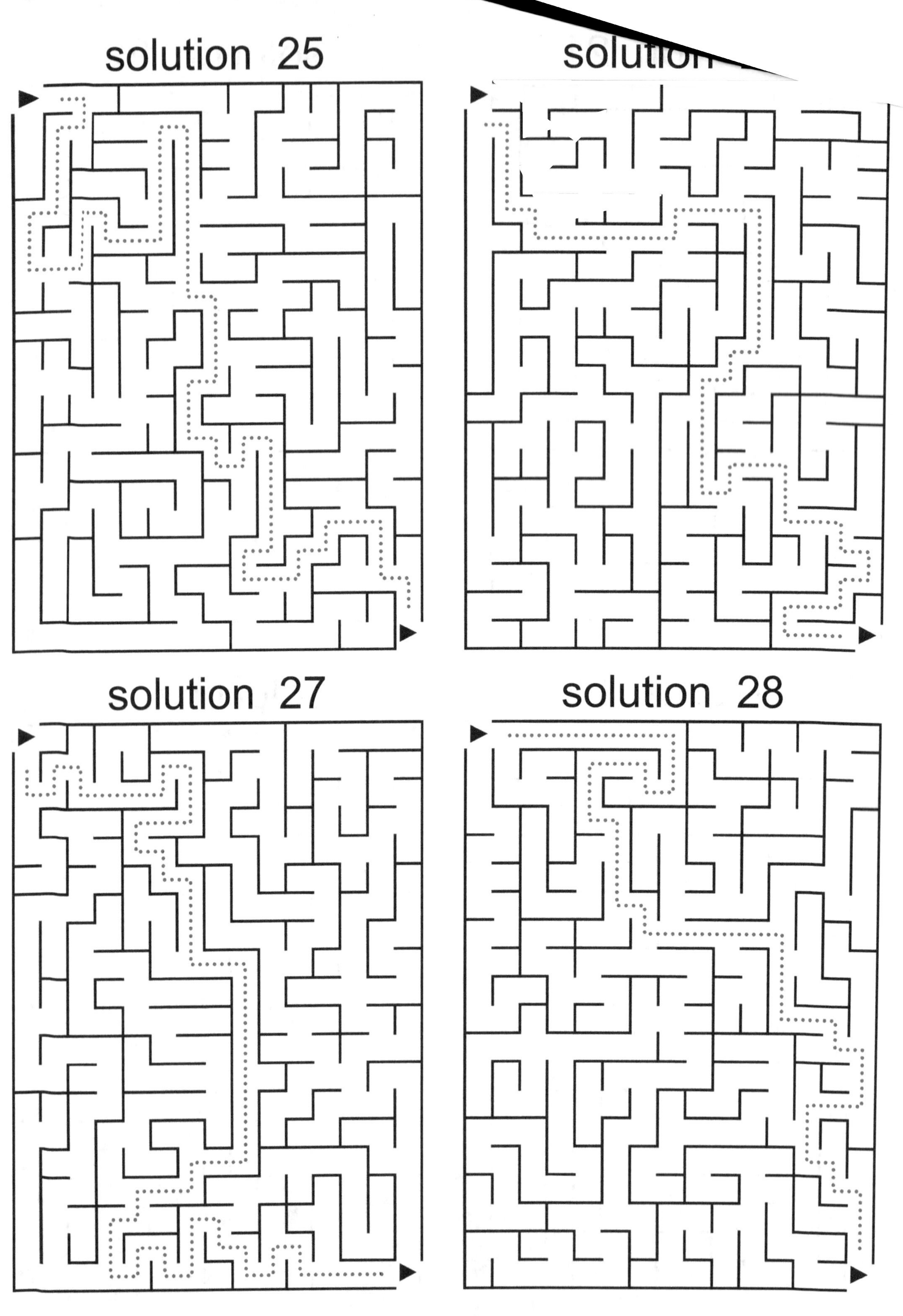

solution 25
solution
solution 27
solution 28

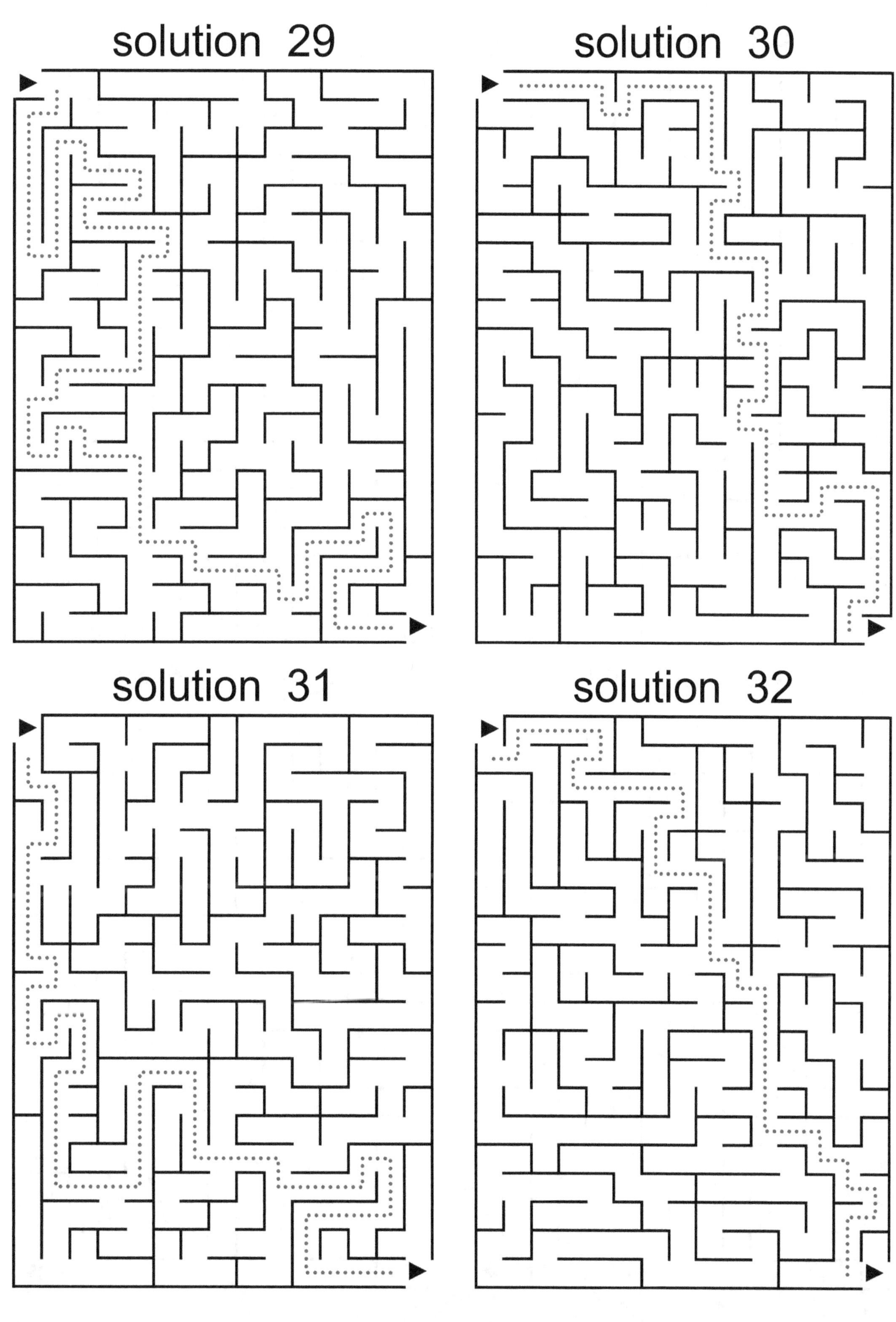

solution 29
solution 30
solution 31
solution 32

solution 33

solution 34

solution 35

solution 36

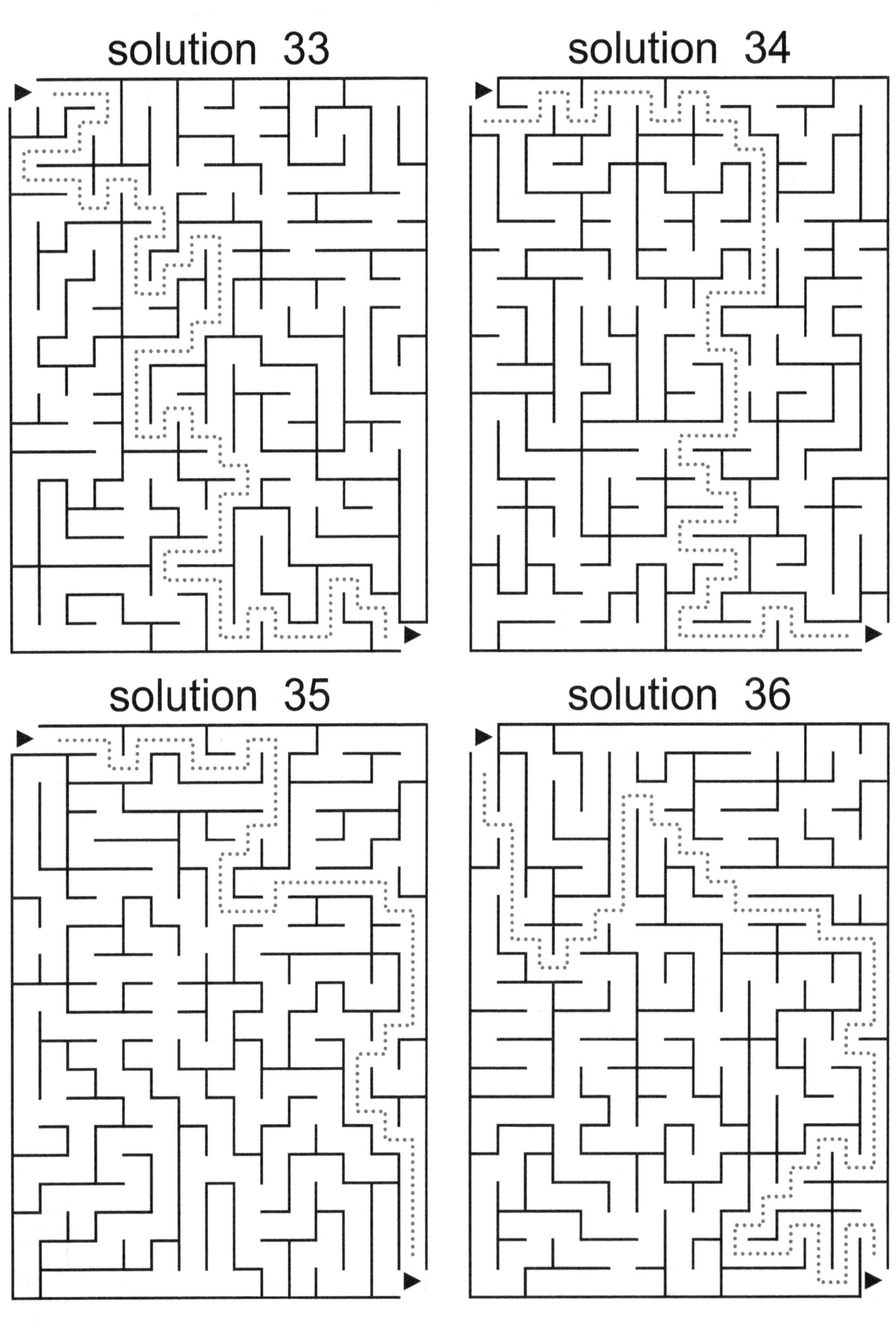

solution 37

solution 38

solution 39

solution 40

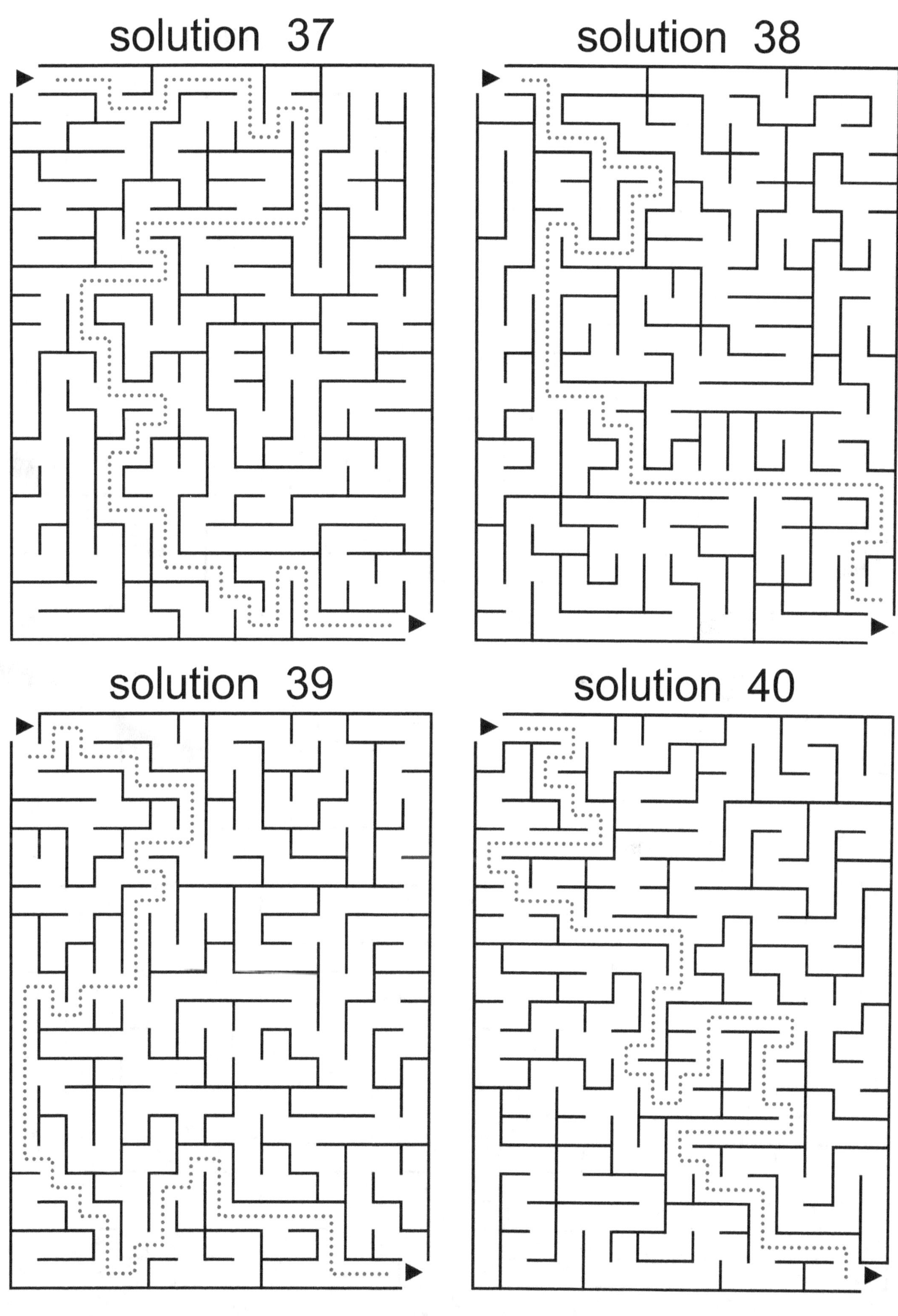

solution 41

solution 42

solution 43

solution 44

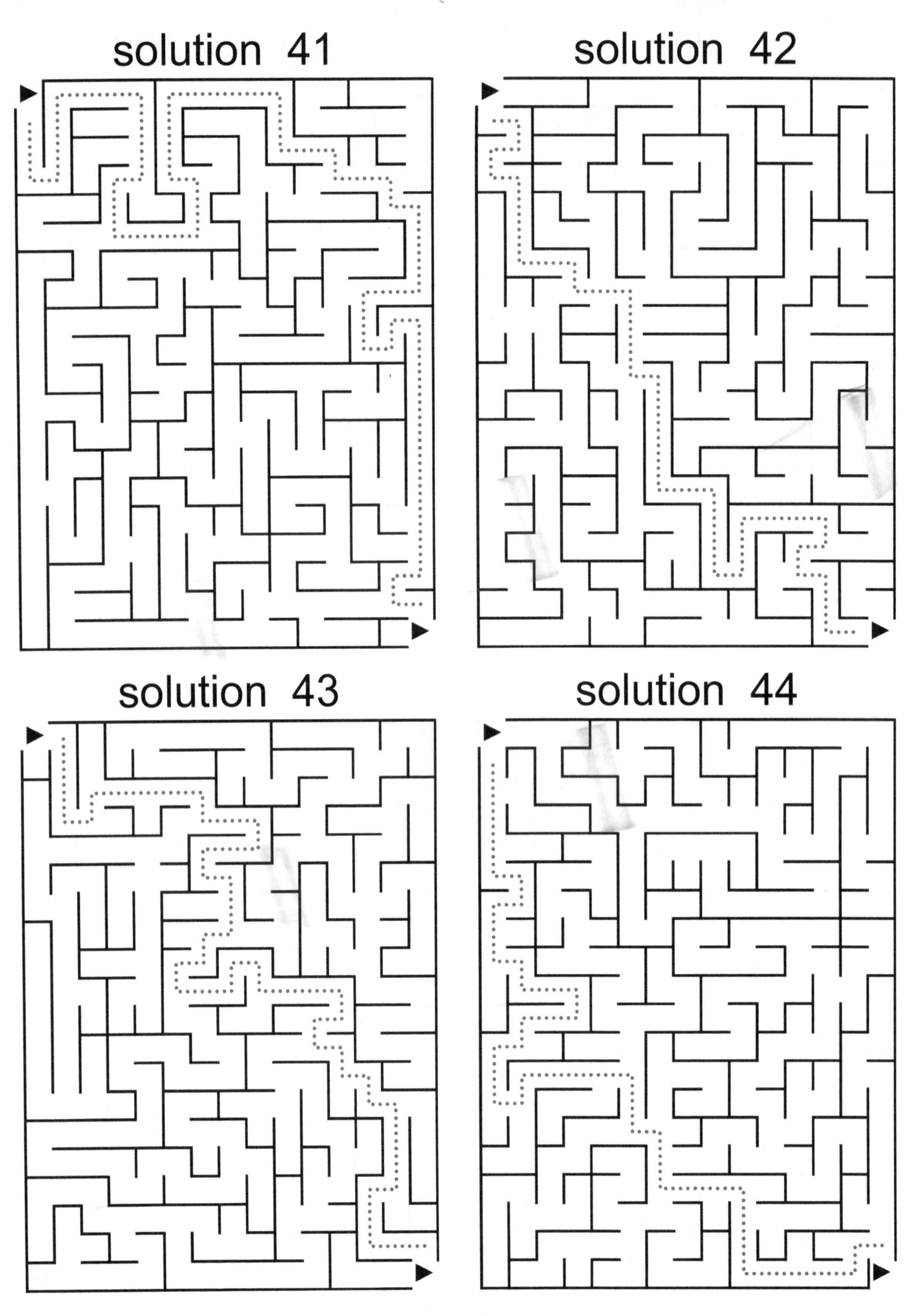

solution 45

solution 46

solution 47

solution 48

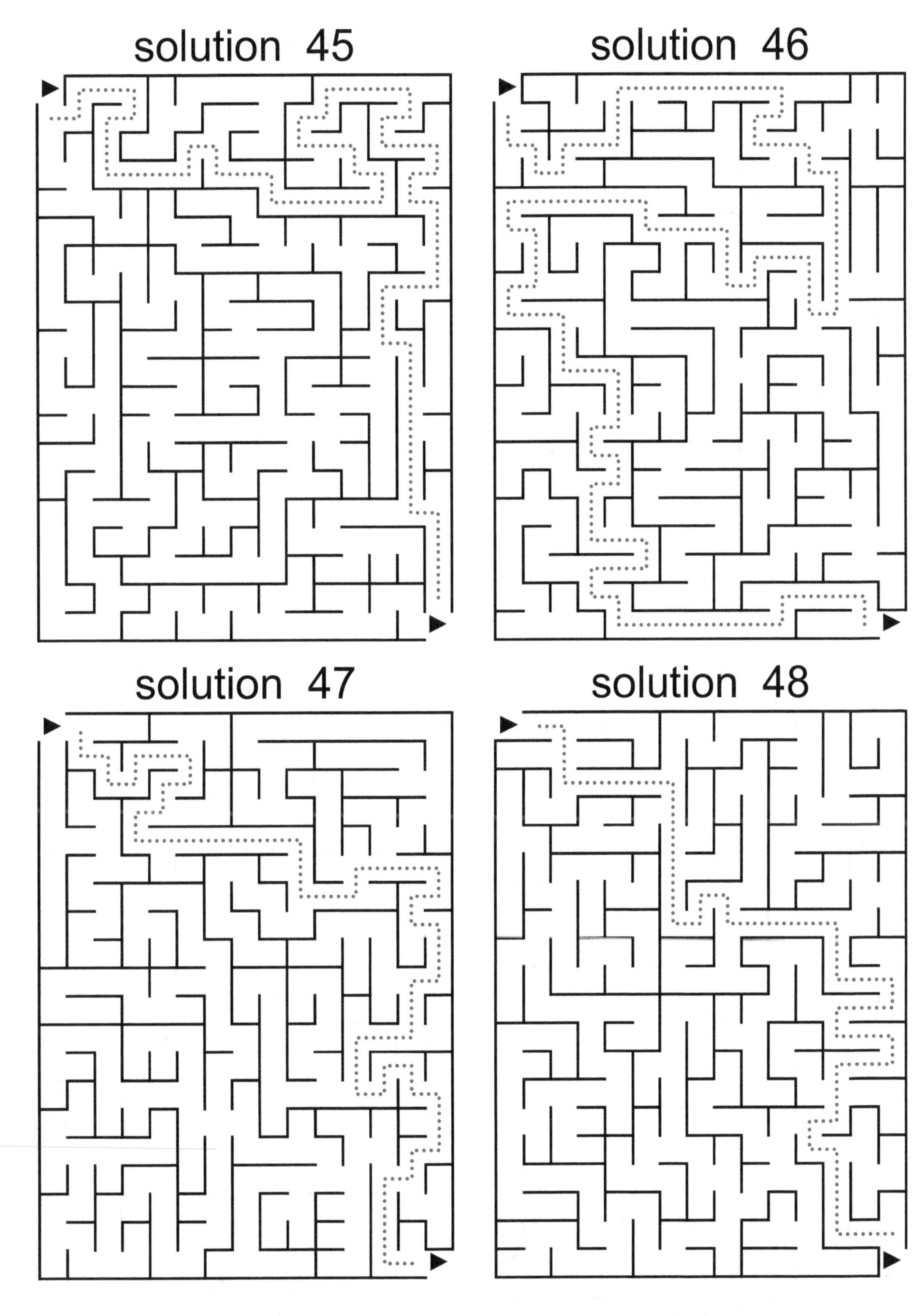

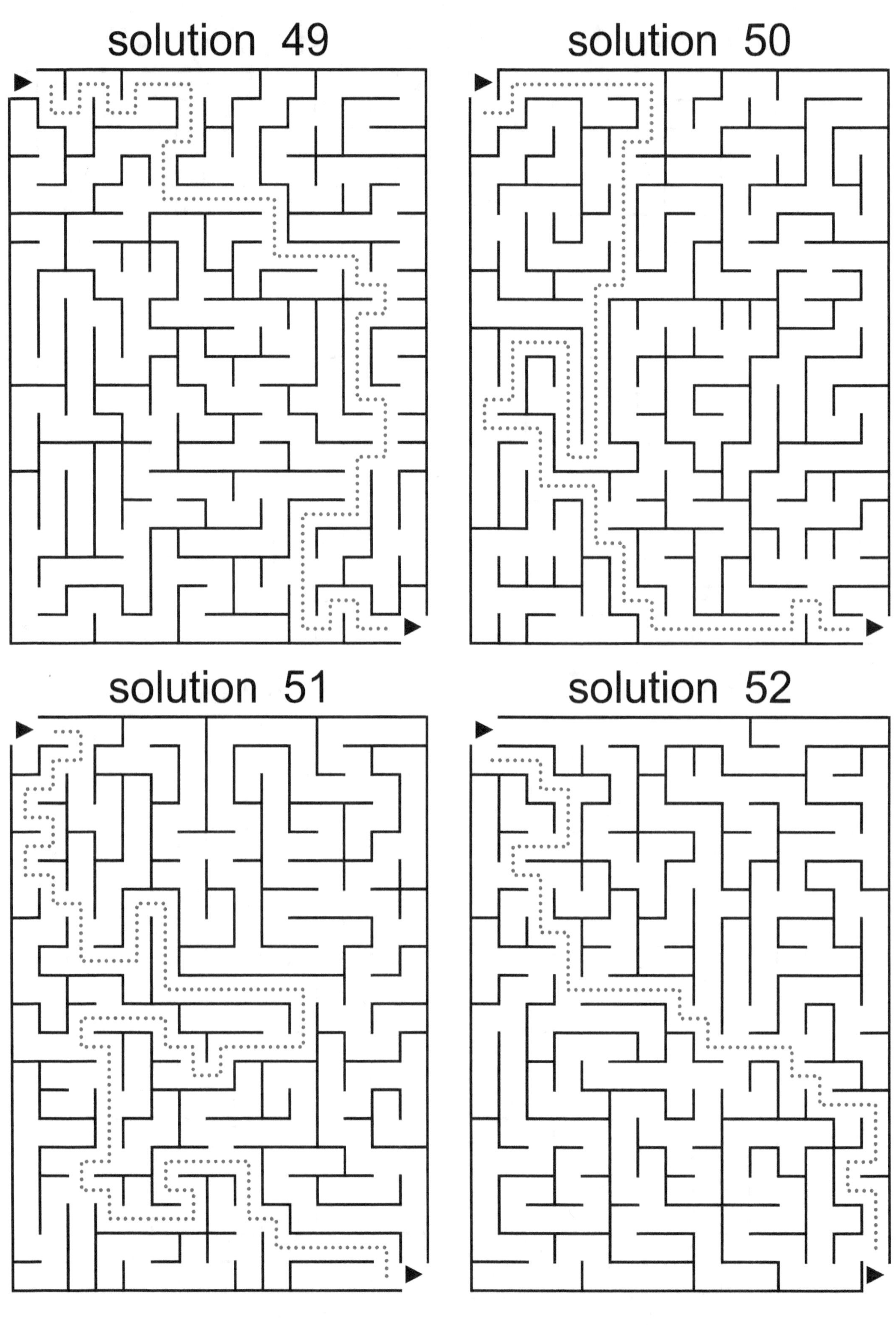

solution 49
solution 50
solution 51
solution 52

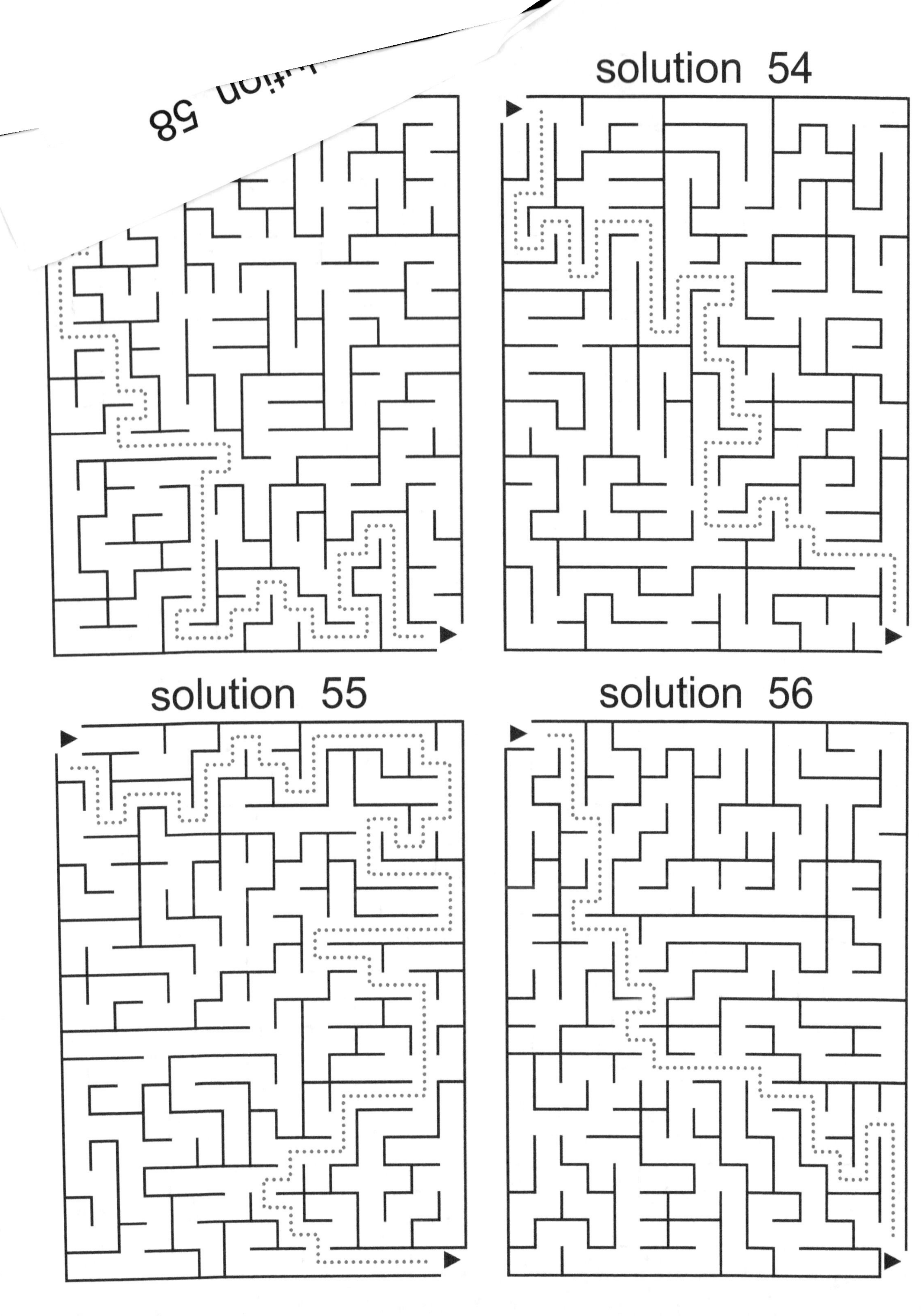

solution 58
solution 54
solution 55
solution 56

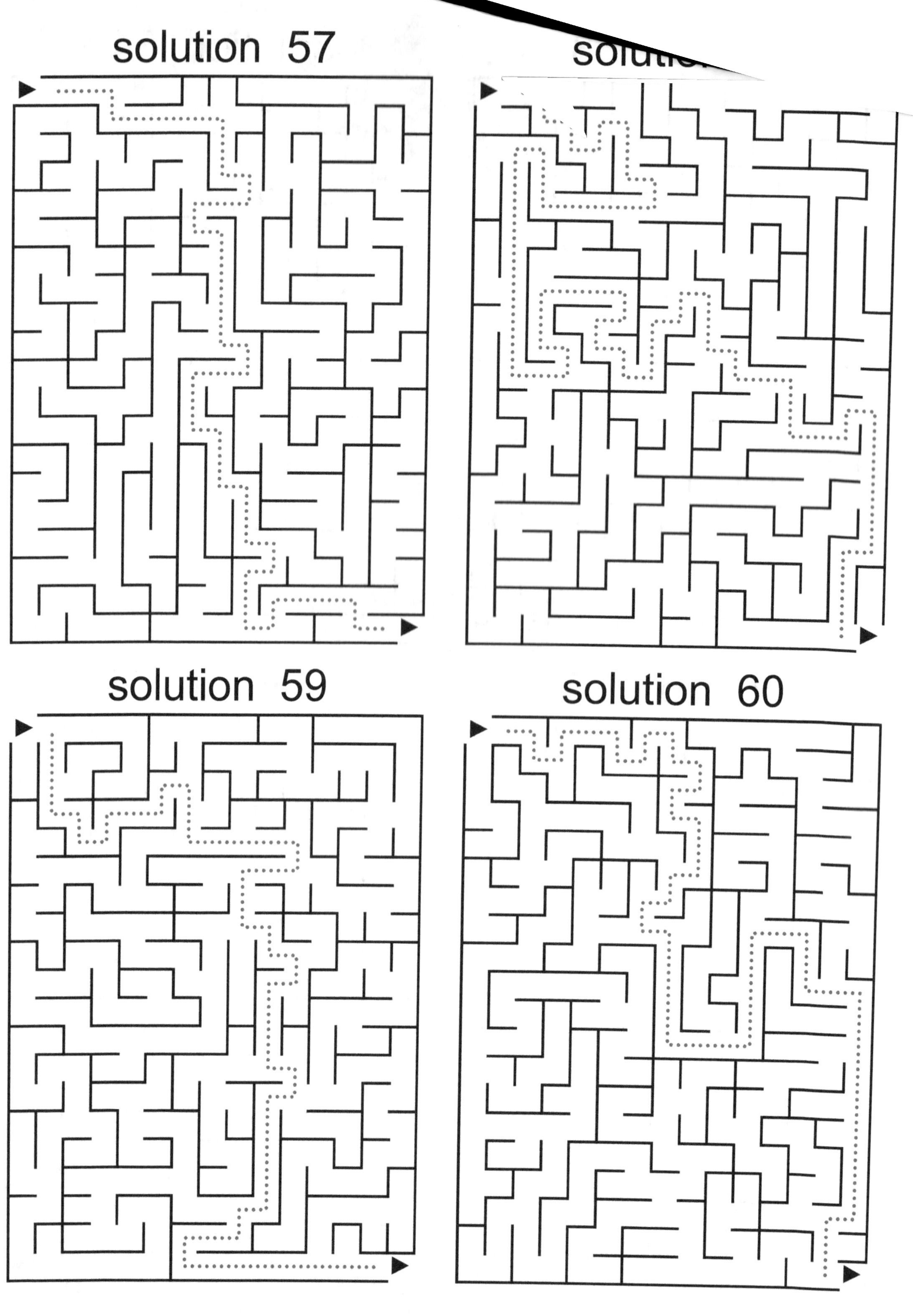

solution 57
solution
solution 59
solution 60

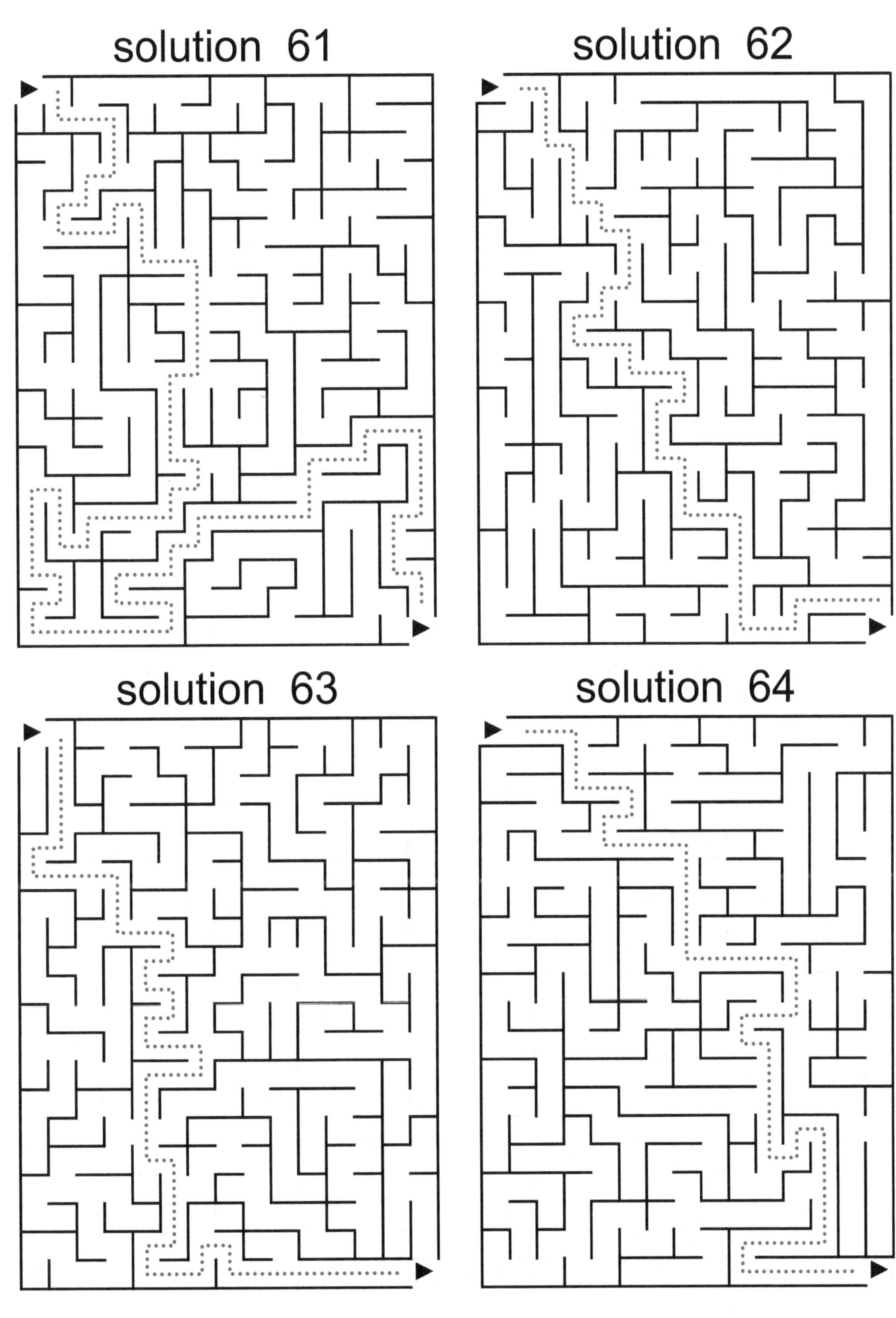

solution 61
solution 62
solution 63
solution 64

solution 65   solution 66

solution 67   solution 68

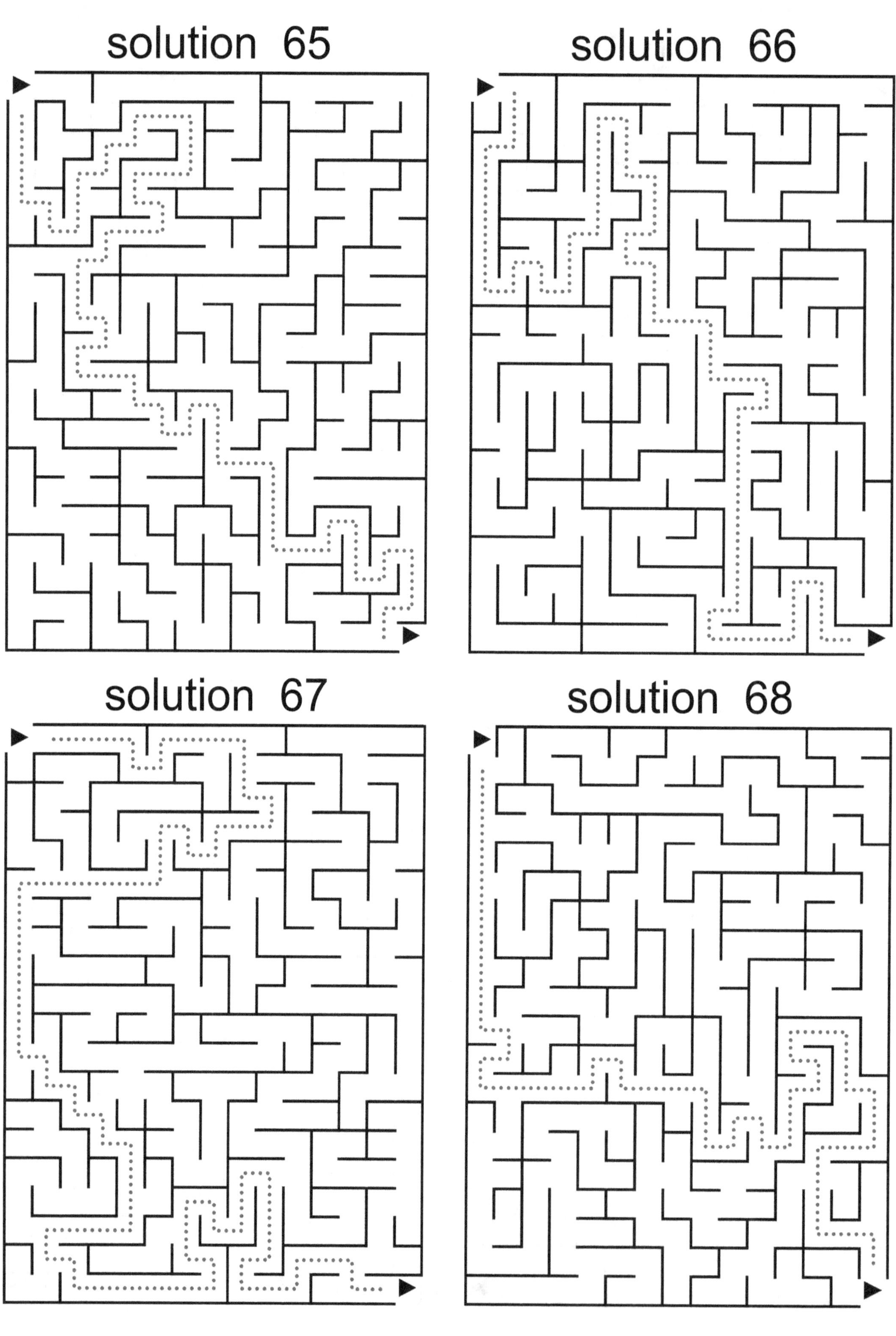

solution 69

solution 70

solution 71

solution 72

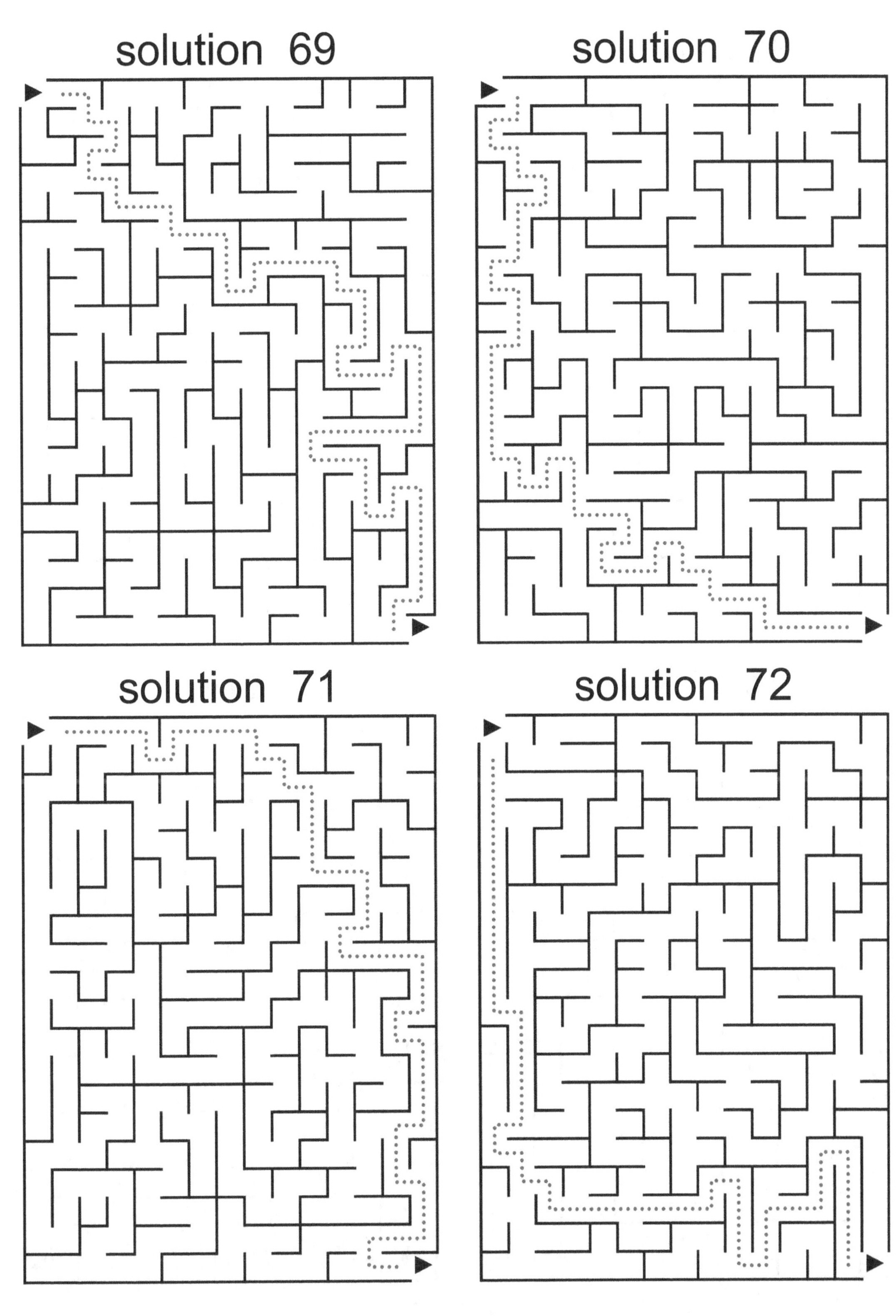

solution 73

solution 74

solution 75

solution 76

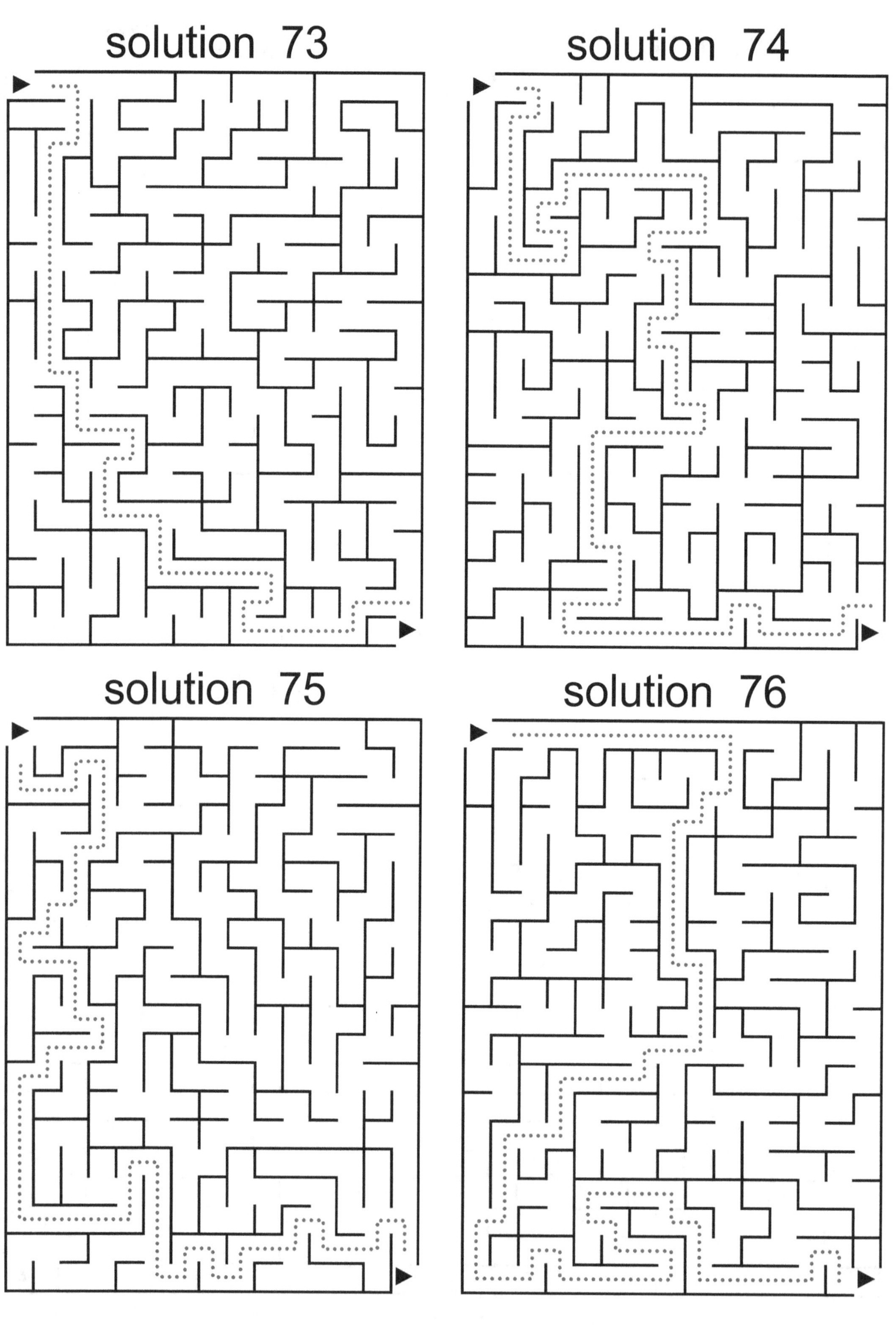

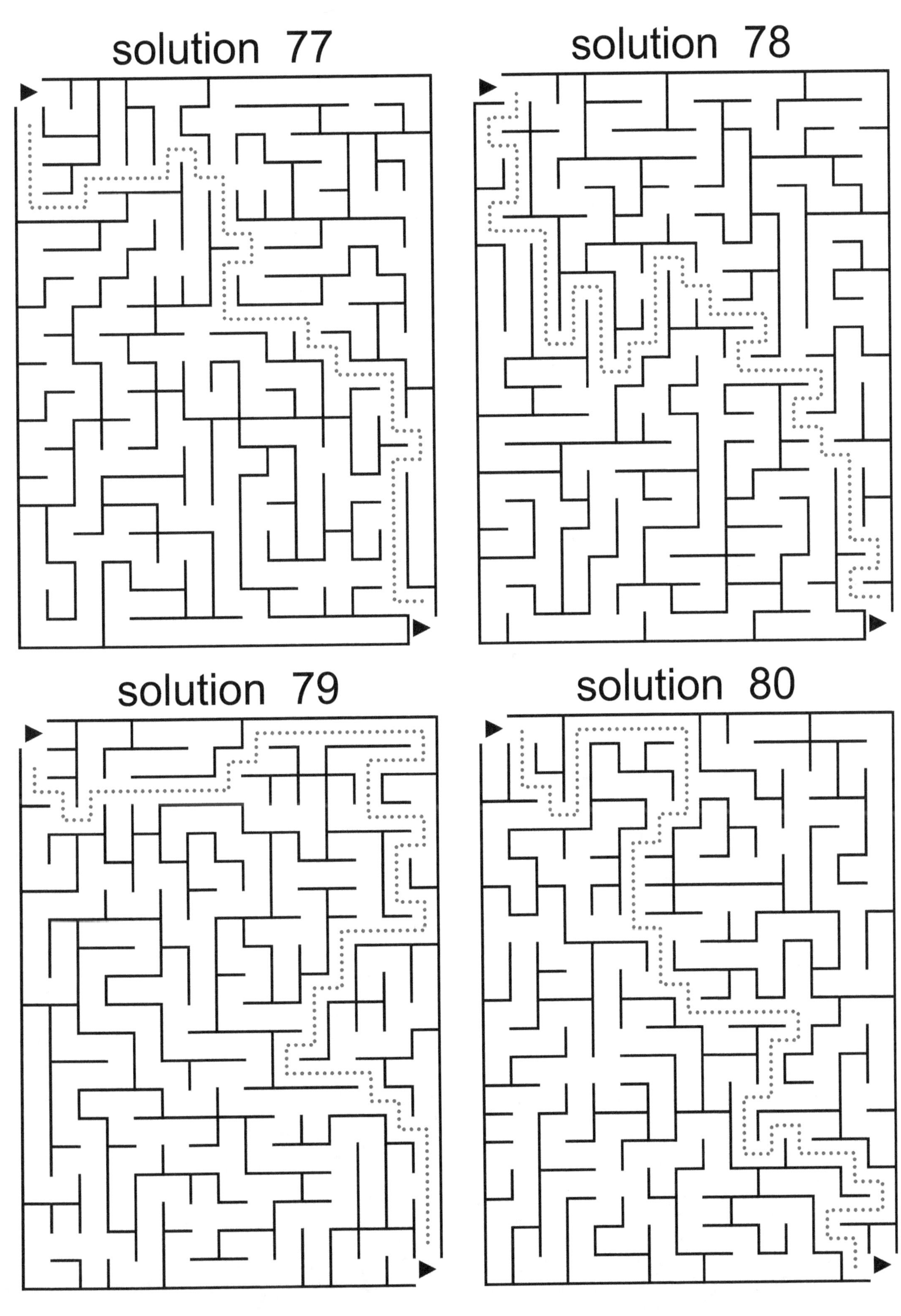

solution 77
solution 78
solution 79
solution 80